How to Close a Sale

How to Close Every Sale Quickly & Easily

By

David Peters

For

The Entrepreneur Skills Institute

Disclaimer

This publication is designed to be used as an information resource only. It is not designed to be used as a definitive plan for closing any specific sales or for use with any specific customer. Since everyone is different and every situation is different, it is not possible for anyone to create a universal or "one size fits all" approach to sales. Therefore it is up to the reader to determine which parts of this book, if any, are applicable to any specific situation or person. The user assumes totally responsibility for the use of or application of any or all parts of this book. The publishers, writers and resellers of this book assume no responsibility for the use or application of any or all parts of this publication.

Contents

Introduction

Closing a sales can be one of the easiest parts of the sales process as long as we do it correctly. Closing a sale is important because it bring us the reward that we have been working towards with our customer. That reward is their willingness to finally complete their purchase.

The closing is where we put everything together. The product, the customer, their problems and how that product is going to solve their problem or address their particular need. If everything has gone well up to this point the closing should be easy. But as we often know, rarely does anything go easy.

In this book we are going to explore how to close a sale quickly, easily and effectively. We will go over what you need to do and, equally important, what you need to stay away from doing. Because sometimes the things we often do causes more damage than the things we don't!

The sales process is an emotional one and we must not only understand the emotions of the customer but how to use them effectively. We are also going to cover that in this book as well. Because once we understand emotions, the entire closing process becomes much easier.

Unlike some sales books that describe ways to close sales at any cost including deception, trickery and outright lying, we are going to go a different route. A route that we believe is the correct way to sell and create long-term sales relationships with our customers. We are going to describe how you can close a sale by making the customer feel comfortable and confident in their decision. Not because you fool them into thinking that way but because you and the customer have worked hard to find the most perfect product for their needs and application.

With so many sales people and businesses being accused, and often found guilty of deception and illegal practices, it is critical that we use the right approach in closing sales and interacting with our customers. That is exactly what we are going to cover in depth in this book.

You will find several different chapters that are focused on the sales closing process. The first "Sales Closing Basics" is going to give you an overview of the sales process, including the closing as well as other factors that will help you not only close sales better but create a much more positive sales process. That information is critical to your overall success.

The second chapter, "Sales Closing Techniques" is where we will go through many different techniques that will help you close more sales in less time with better overall results. This is the "meat and potatoes" part of the book and you will learn a lot in this chapter.

The third and fourth chapters deal with closing internet sales and effective words and phrases that can be used in the closing process. This information is important because internet sales are closed differently and whether your sale is face-to-face or on the internet words are still hugely important.

When you complete the book you should have a complete and in-depth knowledge of how to close sales effectively in pretty much any situation. At that point all you need to do is start using the techniques we give you and practice them. Refine them and integrate them into your own sales style and personality. Not all of them will be a great fit but don't worry about that. There are so many different techniques you are certain to find a few that work perfectly for you.

Before we get started, a word about how this book is designed and structured.

We have been writing sales and business training books for years and have developed a very effective style and format of writing.

We understand that sometimes people reading these types of books do not start at the beginning. There might be an urgent need that needs to be addressed or a topic that has a special interest behind it. Whatever the reason might be, some readers will start in the middle of the book and in some books this presents a problem.

The problem with those books is that when you start in the middle of a book you might miss critical information that was covered prior to where you started and that information is important to understanding the material. But you won't have that problem in this book.

That is because we designed this book in such a way that every chapter can be used as a standalone book that contains all the information you need to understand what is being covered in that particular chapter. So you can start anywhere you want and be able to fully understand what is being discussed.

Because of this certain information might be repeated in the book but that is intentional as well. Not only does repeating important information help you learn better and retain it longer, it also helps reinforce some of the most important information and concepts in the book.

So start wherever you want and address any particular needs you might have. Then, for best results, start back at the beginning and read the book in chapter order.

The book is not long and you should have no problem reading it two or even three times if that is what's needed. Remember, there is no prize or reward for reading through the book in record time. Your only reward should be in the results you get and the knowledge you learned.

Sales Closing Basics

Why People Buy

Before we can efficiently sell someone something, we need to understand why people purchase products in the first place. After all, people must have a reason for spending their hard earned money on a product or service. Understanding the reasons why people purchase helps us determine the proper method of closing the sale.

In the most basic form, people buy things because they either solve a problem or fulfill a need. Solving a problem might mean helping them do something faster, easier or better or enable them to resolve an issue in their life.

Tools are a perfect example of solving problems. If you have a piece of wood that needs to be cut, a saw will address that problem.

If you never are going to need to cut a piece of something, you likely won't ever buy a saw even though the saw might be great and the price amazing. If you don't have a need, you are not likely to buy the product.

Fulfilling a need is slightly different but involves the same process. If you have a need or desire to go on vacation to Hawaii you will look into trips to Hawaii and purchase one. If you don't want to go to Hawaii, you won't. The difference with needs and desires is that most of the time these are not necessity purchases. In other words, while you would like to have them you do not have to have them. You can live without them.

As far as purchasing products are concerned, the stronger the need or desire and the more important or severe the problem is, the more likely the customer is to complete their purchase.

For example, I might like to buy a new suit because my old suit is worn out. If I don't have a need for a suit right now, I might wait for a sale or just wait to save the money. But if I have a big job interview next week, I would be more likely to get the suit now to wear it on a job interview.

I might want to change the washers on my bathroom faucet as well but since I don't enjoy doing that I might wait.

But if the washer breaks and water is pouring out the faucet and I can't turn it off I will be much more agreeable to purchasing the tools and parts that I need.

There is one other reason people buy things and that is to make their lives easier or to be able to get something done faster. Products that make things easier and faster are usually very good sellers as long as the issue they address is a common one.

There are detergents that clean wash better in less time while using less water. No one drives a screw by hand anymore. They use a cordless screw gun instead. Power lawnmowers cut faster and easier than the old push models. The list can go on and on but if something makes a task easier and faster to complete, customers are usually at least interested.

This is a very high overview of why people buy products. There are many more details but these are the three primary motivators. Address any or all of these during closing and you will increase your chances of closing the sale.

It is important that you understand why people want or buy certain products so you can discover things about the customer and the product and bring them together during the closing process. If you can link a specific customer need to a particular product, the customer will then see that this product will do what they wanted and sometimes more.

You cannot hope to close a sale if you do not correctly identify the need. Then, once you identify the need, you can take steps to magnify that need, create more urgency where little might exist and get the customer more in the mood to buy.

Some people think that really good salesmen just have the magic words that force a customer to purchase products they might not need. That simply is not true. What great closers usually have is the ability to show the customer that the product they are interested in will address their specific needs.

They will have a way with words but only because they chose their words carefully so that they connected the customer to the product. This is not brainwashing or anything like that. It is just helping the customer realize and understand that this product will do what they want, and hopefully more, and will either solve a problem, fulfill a need or make their life better.

Very often a customer who doesn't buy is just a customer who doesn't see the connection between their needs and the product. Once that is pointed out to them, they often turn from customer to buyer very rapidly. Making that connection, and making sure the customer understands why the product is perfect for their needs, is the closer.

I urge everyone reading this book to study more on the psychology of buying so that they can gain more insight into why people purchase the products and services they buy every day. For those who are interested in this sort of thing it can be fascinating reading.

As a salesperson, it just makes sense to understand the reasons and impulse behind the purchase process so you can integrate them more into your presentation and closing process. The more you can connect with the homeowner the more you can deliver a presentation that wipes away doubt and confusion and replaces those things with an urge to buy.

Why a Sale Needs to Be Closed

Some people wonder why a sales should need to be closed in the first place. After all, if a person is ready to buy they will buy. If they are not ready we should not force them to commit before they are ready. While that makes sense on some levels, it fails to take into consideration a few basic things when it comes to how customers think.

There are a certain percentage of people who find it very hard to actually commit to purchasing something. They are always finding an excuse to postpone purchasing whatever they need. Sometimes this comes from past experiences where they were burned because they acted too quickly and sometimes it is just because while they need something, they just don't want to spend the money for it.

Whatever those reasons might be, they need to be addressed, brought out into the open and made to go away.

That is the job of the closer. To wipe out hesitancy and procrastination and get the sale made now instead of later.

The problem with waiting until later is that the customer might never come back to you for their purchase. Instead they keep looking and finally, while they are somewhere else, someone will come in, talk to them and close the sale for that business instead of yours!

Very few people will spend the time and effort to come back to you when they are already somewhere else that has the same product at roughly the same price. After all, they are there now, the product is in stock, and the price is the same as your price. So what incentive do they have to come back?

It is up to the closer to have all the answers, ask all the right questions and make all the right statements to convince that customer to purchase now while they are in your store. This is what closers do. They find a way to close the sale before you walk out and look somewhere else.

Here are some of the customer types that need a closer to come in and help finalize the sale:

"Wafflers"

Some customers are never really ready to purchase. They are always looking for a better price or a different model or a different feature or something else that they think they need that might not even exist.

So they keep searching and looking but never make a purchase.

These customers need someone to come in and answer their questions, reassure them about the products capabilities and its ability to do what they need it to do and to assure them that this is the right product for them. Once that is done they need one final "nudge" to get them to purchase.

There is nothing wrong with that approach as long as you are trying to close a sale for the right product for that customer. As long as the customer is getting what they need or want, a gentle nudge and some reassurance is all that many customers need to turn them into a buyer. Without that nudge and reassurance they might never buy anything.

"Price Hunters or Deal Seekers"

These are the customers who are always looking for the best deal and they have no problem waiting for the next big sale, search all over town for the best price or wait until the new models come out for better pricing on the older ones.

These types of customers can be difficult because they are usually suspicious as well. But most of them do their homeowner and will respond to the right deal under the right circumstances.

In these cases the closer will offer them a good price, perhaps throw in a few bonuses or value added extras such as free delivery or free batteries so that overall deal has more appeal. Usually there is an on-going negotiation between customer and closer until a satisfactory deal is reached. Then the deal is closed.

A closer is needed in these deals because these customer need someone to haggle and negotiate with. You cannot do this with a checkout clerk or cashier because they usually to not have the authority to change prices or throw in any extras. A closer does have this authority and knows how to navigate through the process so both the business and the customer wind up happy with the outcome.

"Unsure Customers"

There are a significant number of customers who are never really convinced or satisfied that they have found the best product for their use or application. They will ask endless questions, go to unlimited stores and talk to unlimited people while never really making a decision.

These customers really need someone to come in and answer their questions and remove their fears. That is the job of the closer who should be skilled in not just product knowledge but in customer service as well.

There will always be the customer or two who is never satisfied and you cannot do anything about that. But a good closer will be able to turn many of these hesitant customers into buyers with the right answers and the right approach.

"Suspicious Customers"

There are customer who are always suspicious of anyone who tried to sell them anything and to a certain extent, I am also one of those people. There are so many crooks and scammers out there, as well as outlandish marketing claims and promises, that many people often have no idea whether they are being lied to or actually helped.

You cannot blame them and you can understand why they feel that way but that is not going to help you close the sale. What will help you is being able to gain the customers confidence and get them to really believe you. If you are being honest with the customer and selling them the right product for the right application and giving them a good deal in the process, you need to communicate that with them.

A good closer will relate to the customer and express empathy to them and try to honestly gain their confidence. Not through deceit or lies but through actually taking their best interests to heart and helping them to the best of their abilities.

Being honest and truthful with customers will not only help you close sales now but will also help you establish a great reputation which is going to help you close more sales tomorrow as well. Customers do not exist in a vacuum and treating one very well today is going to be shared with a lot of other customers tomorrow.

"Techno-Phobes"

Techno-phobes come in two types. We have the one who is afraid of technology and feels that it is somehow too complicated for them to learn. Many older customers fall into this group. This is more intimidation and fear than anything else.

The second group of techno-phobe are those customer who want to buy something today but are always afraid that the product they buy today will become obsolete tomorrow. In some industries such as phones and computers, this can be a legitimate concern when new technology changes every year or so. After all, no one wants to buy an expensive product today only to find out that it is outdated and obsolete in 2 months.

Both of these fears are legitimate and understandable but at the same time they should not stand in the way of people getting what they want in life. No matter when you buy there is always going to be something new coming down the road a bit. The challenge is getting rid of the fear.

The closer can do this by making sure the customer understands that just because a new model is coming out does not make the existing models obsolete. They can talk about the new models costing more or having features that this customer does not need. They can talk about how even though a new model might be coming out next year the old model will still be supported and will continue to function at a high level.

This is just another example of a closer addressing a fear, teaching the customer how to deal with that fear and getting them to make a commitment. It is not as easy as it seems but not as hard as some might think it is.

That fact is, some customers need that extra push or nudge to make a decision. Customers often get lost in "information paralysis" where they are so consumed with getting all the information that they lose the ability to just make a decision. When this happen we need an outside party, in this case the closer, to lead them through everything and help them make that decision.

Again, this works only when the salesman has the right motives and is honestly trying to help the customer to the best of his or her ability. That means choosing the right products for the customer and presenting them in the best possible light so the customer completely understands that this is the right product for them.

When you are able to get a customer to that point, it is a piece of cake to close the sale. It's getting to that point that is the really hard work at times. But it can be done.

And it often needs to be done to get the sale.

Why the Opening Sets Up the Closing

One common misconception is that a salesman can swoop in at the last minute and act like the hero closing every deal with an easy flourish that thrills customers right and left. The reality is that the closer is just the last part of a situation that has been developing over time.

People tend to buy from people and businesses where they get the best experience. Very often prices is not the motivating factor but the overall experience is. Customers want to feel appreciated, needed and they want their needs and demands addressed. If you can achieve that you have a great chance of closing more sales both with and without a closer!

In reality, the person charged with closing the sale is just another person trying to build upon what hopefully has been a very positive experience up to that point in time.

If the experience has not been very positive, or if it has been negative in any way, there is little hope that any closer will be able to salvage the situation.

The closer builds upon the framework that has already been created. Sometimes this framework is not strong or positive enough to result in a sale. So the job of the closer is to come in, assess what has already been done and then build upon that adding value and encouragement, until the sale is made.

It is kind of like pushing a rock up an incline and you are almost there but not quite, and you have someone walk over to help you with one last punch to get it over the edge. The closer is the one giving that one last push.

But let's say you only were able to move that rock up the incline only about a quarter of the way up. Over you had it higher and then it rolled back and you had to start over. In those cases you will need more than one last push. You will need a series of pushes.

In the sales process, we have to go through several stages before we even get close to the point of closing the sale. We have to identify the customer's needs, choose the right products, present them to the customer, give them choices and suggestions, gain their confidence, answer their questions and many other things.

Every time we do something right and it is viewed positively by the customer it is like pushing that rock up a little higher. Every time we do or say something negative in the eyes of the customer that rock falls back a bit. Depending on just how important or how negative things might be, that rock might fall a little bit, roll all the way down, or roll all the way down and out to the parking lot where it gets in its car and drives away!

In order for a closer to be effective, they have to step into extremely positive situations where the customer has been treated very well up to that point. Then the closer can capitalize on all those positives and provide that extra little push to seal the deal.

To give every sales person the highest chance to close deals and make sales, provide them the product and sales training they need to provide a first class customer experience for every customer. Not just a few customers but every single customer that walks through your doors. Because the customer that doesn't buy today just might come back to purchase tomorrow.

And they might just tell their friends as well.

Connecting the Dots

Though this might seem a little condescending towards our customers, the fact remains that we cannot leave it up to the customer to see all the benefits and reasons why they should purchase a particular product. It is not that they are not smart enough to do so, it is just that they are often just not aware that such things exist.

Very few things can be as frustrating as having a customer walk out the door because they did not realize that the product they were looking at was perfect for their needs. When this happens both the customer and the business loses. The customer doesn't get the right product for their needs and the business loses a sale that might possibly go to someone else.

Good salesmen do not leave it up to the customer to see all the features, advantages and benefits of a particular product as far as their customer is concerned. They will craft a presentation where they go through things one by one and help the customer "connect the dots" between their particular needs and the product in question.

This is not any kind of "hard sell" or anything like that. It is more of an education process where we lead the customer through a kind of discovery process. During this process we not only point out what the product does but we also let the customer know what this means for them.

Features are one thing but when we take a feature and turn it into a personal benefit that the customer can related to, that is where the connection is made and the customer becomes aware of the real value in purchasing that product. The more features and benefits that can be pointed out to the customer the greater the desire to purchase will become.

This usually is done without the customer being aware of the process. Here is an example of a salesman pointing out a feature in such a way that it resonates with the customer:

"One thing I love about this washing machine is it is a high capacity unit. You mentioned you do a lot of wash because you have 4 children. Well this machine with its extra capacity will turn 6 loads of wash into 3 or 4 and save you a lot of time and water as well."

And let's take it a step further:

"Another advantage of the high capacity machine is saving on detergent and bleach as well. It is estimated that the high capacity and high efficiency design will save the average user roughly $100 a year in detergent and bleach. With your 4 children I wouldn't be surprised if you save even more. That means that over the life of the machine you will save a lot more than you originally paid for it!"

In that example we took a feature (high capacity) and made it relevant to the needs of the customer (saving time, high amount of usage). We took a feature and made it real in the eyes of the customer. Then, to help seal the deal, we also pointed out that the savings in supplies (detergent and bleach) will more than pay for the washer over its lifetime!

This is not a hard sell and nowhere in the process did you ask for the sale or push for a decision. At this point you are adding positive thoughts and experiences and help the customer make the connection between what they read on a sign and what it will mean for them in their real life.

Connecting the dots helps the salesman make the customer aware of the real benefits and values behind the products. It really helps to upsell a customer to a higher or better model as well. Especially if it will better serve the needs of the customer.

Another area where connecting the dots comes in handy is during the comparison of different makes and models.

While many customers might gravitate to the lower priced models, taking features and connecting them with the customer's needs can help not only justify the larger cost of the higher model but convince the customer that this is a much better option.

The basic rule of thumb her is if you want the customer to be aware of every reason for why they should purchase that particular product right here and now, you have got to lead them by the hand and explain it all to them. It is up to you to make sure they see things from every angle and that you point out everything that they may or may not be aware of.

Here is another way of looking at the same concept:

If a product has features that will really help a customer and they are not aware of them, then those features are meaningless to the customer. The product might as well not have them. As far as convincing the customer to purchase that product over another, only those factors that the customer is aware of will influence or impact their decision.

For example, using the same washer example, if the washer has a "light load" setting that saves 50% on water usage that will mean something to the customer only if you make them aware that this is what "light load" really means.

If you are selling a car and it has an economy mode that saves the average driver $500 a year in gasoline that will help you sell the car only if the buyer is aware of those savings. If you do not mention this to the customer you are doing your customer, and your business a disservice.

Remember that the most effective way to sell any product or service is to sell solutions to a problem. If a customer has a problem, then the salesman needs to connect as many dots as possible between the product and solving that problem. If you can connect dots to solving other common problems as well, then you can really hit a home run.

Like in this example:

"Mr. Smith, you had said you needed a cordless screw gun that will a 4"screw into hardwood. Well this model will easily do that as well as a few other things as well. In addition to driving screws, the two speeds can help you drill hole in steel and wood without chipping. The slower speed works great when you need more control such as installing wall anchors and running a drill operated pump. This is the same price as some of the other models but it will do so much more it just makes sense to choose this one. Just don't tell your wife all the things it can do or she will keep you busy for months!

In this example we told him the product would easily do what he needed it to do but then we described all the other things this particular model could do as well.

We even finished it off with a veiled reference of how many other tasks you could do around the house with this versatile tool.

The more dots we connect between customer and product the greater chance we will have to creating a sale. Customers love value and the love versatility. The love features as well but only when they know and understand what those features will mean to them in their lives.

Not all manufacturer or product claims are accurate or true and when you have personal experience, or when you can draw from comments of previous customers who have used the products, you can save the customer time and money and close more sales. After all, no one wants to get a product home only to find out that it really can't do what it says on the box.

Eighth, and perhaps the most important when it comes to sales and closing, is that product knowledge and experience helps define you as an authority on certain products and services. Because of this you become the "go to" person that customers seek out when they need advice they can count on and believe. Once you get that reputation you really don't have to work very hard to close a sale because your reputation has already done that for you.

You can go a long way with being personable and charming with customers. You can use all the techniques and say all the right things when it comes to closing sales. But actual product knowledge will help you do the one thing that means the most to your customers. It will allow you to provide the information they need to make the right decisions.

And for most customers, that is what they value most of all.

Know Your Customer

Since we are talking about knowledge right now, let's discuss another type of knowledge that is critical to the sales and closing process. That is knowledge of who your customer is and what they are looking for. Without this type of knowledge you cannot possibly serve your customer efficiently and accurately.

Part of the sales and closing process involves taking the product and matching it to the customer. We have already mentioned this a few times. But we cannot possibly match a customer with the right product if we don't know what the customer's real needs are.

Though this might sound a bit funny, or even somewhat condescending, customers often do not know what they really want and it is up to you to discover what that is and use that information to properly guide them to the right product or service for their needs.

Some of the things we need to know about the customer are:

What are they Looking For??

This is just common sense. If you want to be able to help a customer then you have to understand what they are looking for. You need at least some basic information to be able to advise them or at least steer them in the right direction.

We should never allow the customer to proceed blindly because sometimes they are just not knowledgeable in what they are purchasing. So ask questions and keep asking them until you have a pretty good idea what the customer needs.

What is their Problem or Need?

As we have said many times already, every purchase is made to either solve a problem or address a need. Without understanding exactly what that problem or need might be, there is no way we can recommend the right product or service for that issue.

For example, if a customer walks up to you and shows you a bottle of cleaning solution and asks you if it is a good product or not, you would first ask them what they are using it for and what kinds of stains are on which kind of surface. Only then can you really understand what the customer needs and then show them the right products to address those needs.

What Can they Afford or what is their Price Range?

This is important because not everyone has an unlimited budget when it comes to certain items. Understanding what the customer would like to pay can help determine which products are appropriate for their needs.

It can also help determine whether or not financing will come into play or whether financing might be a solution when it comes to recommending a more expensive product because it is a better overall solution.

Understanding finances and budgets will help you save time by recommending products from the beginning that the customer will actually consider purchasing. It will do you little good to preach about how wonderful a certain product is when the customer cannot afford it. When this happens you have just about destroyed any chance of closing a sale.

Do they have any History?

Like it or not, some customers have a history with your business or with a product. This history has a considerable effect on how we need to handle this customer now. Some refer to this history as "emotional baggage" but that is just a fancy name for knowing how the customer feels at this point in time.

For example, if a customer has had problems with your business in the past, then you might have to treat them extra special now to try and restore their faith in you and your business. What we are attempting now is to replace a negative experience with a new positive one. But we can only know the need to do this if we know our customer.

Sometimes we encounter customers with a well-known reputation of being difficult. I am not talking about customers that have legitimate problems or complaints. I am talking about those customers who manufacture problems and have baseless complaint or are, for some reason, never really happy with you or anything else. It is helpful to understand this from the beginning so you understand that no matter what you do it might never be enough.

Sometimes our approach to customers is going to hinge on who they are and what their history is. Sometimes this might not be fair as one customer might get a better or different deal than another but usually this is done for good reason. But in order to understand those reasons we have to know the history behind them.

Taking all of this information and understanding it is not only going to help us understand the customer but also what they are looking for when they walked through our doors or clicked on our website. This is the knowledge we use to make the best recommendation or the most accurate comments.

So many businesses and salespeople concentrate so much on product knowledge that they neglect the customer service side of things and fail to understand their customers. When this happens we run the risk of saying the wrong thing, recommending the wrong product and even selling the customer something that they don't need or a product that will not do what the customer needs it to do.

Remember that selling and closing sales require an in-depth knowledge of BOTH the product AND the customer. The more knowledge we have the best and most accurate decisions we will make. There is a difference between guessing and making an informed decision.

That difference is knowledge.

In both the customer and the product.

Ask Questions

We all love the customers that come in and tell us everything we need to know to choose the right product or fill the right need. But unfortunately many customers just do not offer all the information that we need to make the right choices or decisions. In these cases it is up to the salesman or the closer to ask the right questions.

Obtaining information can be a difficult task with some customers either because they are unwilling to share information or because they just don't know the answers or understand the questions. This does not mean they are not intelligent, it just means they lack the knowledge required to give the right answer. Sometimes, they even possess information that is important but they do not realize it.

In order to get information, we need to ask questions designed to draw out that information. These questions can range from the simple "What are you looking for?" or "How much room do you have to fit this product in?" to more difficult questions such as "What speed hard drive are you looking for?" In order to get this type of information we can ask two types of questions.

The first type of question is called a closed question and the reply is usually a yes or no or possibly a maybe. These questions are used to narrow down or eliminate certain things from the process. They help us make more accurate decisions.

Examples of closed questions are: "Do you want white or black?" or "Is $500 out of your price range?" or "Have you ever used this type of product before?" All of these questions can be answered with a "yes" or a "no".

The second type of question is the open-ended question. These questions are specifically designed to elicit a more detailed and longer response. You usually cannot answer an open-ended question with a yes or a no. You usually have to think about your answer and provide at least a detail or two in that answer.

We use open-ended questions when we are dealing with a customer who is difficult to get information out of. These are the customers who prefer to answer in one word answers and make getting more out of them like pulling teeth. Open-ended questions make them provide details.

Examples of open-ended questions might be: "What happened when you tried this product at home?" or "When the problem happened, what were you doing? Or "What about this product do you like or dislike?"

All of these questions require a response with some kind of detail or information in it. You usually cannot just answer "yes" or "no" although some people will try.

The closer should use these questions to gain more insight into what is going on in the head of the customer. By asking the right questions we can uncover what the reasons for hesitating on purchasing might be. Then once we know the reasons behind the hesitation we can address each issue. Once all the issues have been resolved or wiped away, the sale is made.

Generally, the more questions we ask, the better and more accurate our decisions will be. Think of asking questions as a funnel. In the beginning we are at the top of the funnel with a wide area to hold all the possibilities or choices. Ask we ask more and more questions we move down into the narrower parts of the funnel where the choices or options are fewer and fewer. Finally, we exit the funnel with just one or two possible choices.

Questions should be asked to narrow down choices and further define what the customer really wants or needs. The more we define the more accurate our decisions will be.

But sometimes there is a limit to how far down we can dig for information. Sometimes it is just not possible to get down to just one choice or option.

At this point we just have to make an informed decision using the information we have at our disposal. We cannot continue to ask question after question hoping to have the decision made for us.

Sometimes customers will be determined to keep asking questions and then will suffer from "paralysis by analysis" which refers to having so much information but still needing more before they are willing to make a decision. When we find ourselves, or our customer, in that position we just have to force ourselves to make a decision. An informed decision but a decision none the less.

Questions help us get information that can be important when it comes to resolving a problem or selecting the right product. It is up to the salesman to ask the questions designed to solicit the information. It is not the responsibility of the customer to provide all the information to the salesman.

It certainly would help, but it is still the responsibility of the salesman to ask for it when it is not volunteered.

Creating the Perfect Picture

One of the things that all sales people, and all closers, need to do when trying to sell anything to a customer is try to create the most vivid and life-like image of the customer actually using the product in the mind of the customer.

Buying things is sometimes both a practical and emotional process. The actual purchase doesn't happen until the brain signals that some kind of emotional response and bond have been created between the customer and the product. Until that bond is created, the customer is not likely to buy unless the product being considered is a real necessity.

Whether customers realize it or not they develop feelings and attachment to certain things they buy. It is not something they do on purpose but most of the time something about the product triggers some kind of reaction in their brains.

I am sure that there have been times when you just found that you liked something better than something else. You weren't really sure why but you knew you liked one product better than the other. Something about it was appealing to you. Maybe it was the design or the color or something else but whatever it was your brain reacted to it.

People go car shopping and they don't always buy what is the most practical car or the car that uses the least gas or has the most space. Instead, they buy the make and model that appeals to them the most. They like the color or the way the body looks or maybe the way the driver's seat feels. Whatever the reason, they buy it because they like it.

Good closers understand this and seek to establish that same kind of connection and appeal with the products that they are trying to sell. They try to create a mental picture in the mind of the customer that shows them using the product and enjoying it or getting whatever benefit from the product that they can.

This is important because the more the customer can imagine them using and liking the product, the more likely they are to purchase it. So they question now should be "How do we create such a picture in the mind of the customer?"

A closer can help the customer imagine what life would be with that product as part of it. They can point out the uses and the benefits and how life would be better if they purchased that product. They can point out how the customer could spend all the extra time they would have now that the product is making something faster and easier. They could have the customer imagine playing gold instead of mowing the lawn or fitting into a smaller sized pair of pants after using their new treadmill for a month or two.

They might say something like this to the customer:

"Imagine how different your Saturday's are going to be once you have this riding lawnmower. You will cut your mowing time in half and you can use that extra time to play with the kids or get an earlier round of golf in before lunch. Just having that extra time, and not feeling quite so tired, is why most people purchase these mowers."

In that example the salesman has helped paint a picture of a more relaxing day where the customer gets to do more of the things that they want and be less tired and have more energy. All of those things are positives and help paint a very pleasant picture in the customer's mind.

Whatever approach you take it should help the customer create a positive image in their minds of that product. That images should be as clear and vivid as possible. You accomplish that by pointing out more and more positive things about that product and how it will benefit that customer.

Be specific and be descriptive. Concentrate on the positive aspects of owning that product and what that product can do for the customer. If it makes life easier, explain why and how it does that. If it makes things go faster, describe how that makes life more enjoyable. Just create the most vivid and positive image in their minds.

What will happen is that the more positive things you point out about that product the stronger the connection becomes between the customer and that product. When the connection becomes so strong that the customer must have it that is when the sale is made.

This is something that often happens I the background without the customer ever being aware of it. But when the sales person is aware of it and does their part in creating that picture, the process happens much faster and closing the sale becomes that much easier.

Involving the Customer

Here is a very effective way of getting the customer to support your suggestions and follow you directions. Get the customer involved in the process and get them engaged in the process. Whenever you make the customer part of the process you will be far more likely to get the result you are looking for.

It is usually easy to get the customer involved no matter where you are in the sales process. In the beginning you can get them involved by simply asking them what they came in for or how you can help them. In the middle of the process you can ask them how they feel about a certain model or suggestion and get their input. This helps in two ways.

First, it makes the customer feel part of the process. This gives them a sort of emotional investment in the process and the feeling that their needs and opinions count and really matter. When they feel they are part of the process they are often more comfortable with whatever the outcome is even if it wasn't what they expected or hoped for!

Second, whenever you make the customer part of things you solicit information from then and this information can help you make better and more accurate decisions. You would be surprised how much you can learn from these kinds of exchanges between you and the customer.

Customers might tell you that they like this product or that one and why and you can use this information to see what is really important to them. This in turn can help you suggest the types of products that are more of what the customer wants. This enables you to not only save time but also help you select products that are going to be much easier for you to sell.

The one area where customer involvement really helps is when there are problems, disagreements or confrontations. Perfect examples of these situation would be on complaints, returns, or warranty claims. These are situations where customers might be angry or have certain expectations of demands that cannot be met.

Part of the problem resolution process involves negotiation and whenever we make customers an active part of that process we usually have better results. We ask them what they are looking for and give them certain options or choices that they can make.

Since they made the choices they will be more receptive to agreeing with them. After all, being part of the decision making process is much better than being dictated to.

As far as the sales closing process is concerned, making the customer part of this works well too. We can ask them about their concerns and issues that are keeping them from purchasing. Then, armed with that information we can take action to address those concerns and issue and try to remove them.

We can also take those concerns and ask the customer how we can resolve those concerns and make them go away. Maybe that might mean a different return policy or a longer warranty or some other thing that we might never have thought of.

Getting the customer involved will also give us insight on what is really important to them. Knowing what is important to the customer not only will help us resolve problems but also help us identify items that will really make them want to buy and buy now.

This is all about communication and any communication is always better when it is a two way process. When one person is always doing all the talking and making all the decisions things do not usually work out very well. But when both parties work together sharing information and thoughts, the end result are usually much better and arrived at much faster.

Well, hopefully these sales basics as related to selling and closing of sales have got you thinking in the right direction. Remember that sales is a practical and emotional process and in order to have the best chances of success we have to address both the practical and emotional components in order to have the best chances of success.

With that in mind, let's move on to the various techniques you can make to close more sales in less time with less effort and higher customer satisfaction.

Switching Roles

Sales is all about the interaction between the customer and the salesman. If that interaction is positive and well received, the likelihood of completing a sale will go way up. If the interaction goes poorly, or if the wrong things are said, the customer might just walk out the door.

So how can we have the best chance of saying and doing the right thing?

The easiest way to is to a bit of internal "research" and place yourself in the position of the customer and figure out how you might react if the same things were said or done to you. Since you are a person like your customers are, your reactions are likely going to be pretty similar to theirs.

This is especially useful when it comes time to determine which words to use or which approach to take. If you react positively to a certain phrase or word, then your customer might react in the same way. But if you react negatively, or if it sounds wrong to you, it is a better idea to rethink your choice of words.

A good practice is to say what you are thinking about saying to your customer to yourself first. Gauge your reaction and see if there are any changes you can make to the words you used to get a more positive result. Continue refining until you have the wording or phrase that you think is best.

Another time switching roles will come in useful is when you are trying to determine which the best course of action to take is. Running through all the available options and then choosing the one that you think is the best is a pretty good starting point as well.

Looking at everything through the customer's eyes is one of the most effective ways of judging a reaction and allowing yourself to make changes without risking the relationship with the customer. It is something every sales and service person should do routinely. You will find yourself catching more mistakes before your customer is ever aware of them!

Sales Closing Techniques

Since everyone is different and every situation is different as well, there is no one perfect way to close a sale. Instead, there are many ways to accomplish closing a call and there will be new ones developed over time. The key is not to try to develop the perfect closing approach but instead to handle each situation differently.

That means evaluating both the situation and the customer and trying to decide which particular approach will have the best chance for success. Sometimes we can combine techniques to increase their effectiveness and address all the concerns.

In this chapter we will cover many of the most common and most effective ways to close a sales call or sales experience.

These are listed in no particular order so do not think that just because something is listed first that it is the most important. (Well, in THIS particular case that happens to be true but after the first one, everyone is equally important!)

Provide Solutions to Problems

This is something that should always be at the forefront of every part of the sales process including the closing. Above all we must always focus on the problems that the product is solving or the need or desire that the problem addresses. If we fail to do this the customer really has no reason to purchase the product at that time.

The more urgent we can appear to make the need or the more serious we can make the problem seem to the customer the more pronounced the need to purchase will be. Don't go overboard or seem to be exaggerating or the customer will see right through that but if you can make the problem appear more severe that will help close the sale.

If the product addresses multiple problems or needs be sure to highlight those as well. The customer might not have those needs but they just might and this can help seal the deal. Addressing multiple problems or multiple needs can often help justify purchasing a higher model or pay a higher price.

There is a direct correlation between perceived value and price so it makes sense to make the product appear more valuable in the eyes of the customer. The more it does, the more valuable it becomes.

Peace of Mind

Many products and services revolve around peace of mind. People purchase extended warranties and protections plans because they want the peace of mind that comes from knowing that if something breaks they will be covered. They will pay a nice price for that peace of mind.

People will pay more for products with great reputations or products that are extremely well built as well. Any time you can point out exceptional reliability and longevity that will be a positive as far as the product is concerned.

Some products are designed for peace of mind such as fire alarms and other safety protects or personal security products. Try to reinforce the peace of mind aspect of the product without frightening the customer in the process.

For example, you might mention to a customer thinking about purchasing a smoke detector or alarm that advanced warning not only saves lives but also allows the homeowner to address the issue faster thus limiting the damage. Anything you can do to point out the advantages as they pertain to peace of mind will help close the deal.

Remain Seated

This is more of a body language factor than anything else but if you are talking to the customer in a seated position, do not get up. Getting up could signify an end to the conversation or provide the customer with an easier opportunity to exit the conversation.

Remain seated where your customer is more of a contained presence and will be more in your control. In this position the customer is more likely to be concentrating on what you have to say as well.

If Appropriate, Create a Proposal In Writing

Though this might not apply to every situation, creating a proposal in writing will provide the customer with a document outlining all the details to the offer and the product as well. This can come in handy when you are offering special add-on bonuses or benefits that are numerous or might be difficult to remember. Very often these get lost in the process and might not be taken into consideration when evaluating your offer against others.

The possible downside to providing a written document is that the customer might take that to another business and ask them to match it or beat it.

Companies that offer that service often require a written document and will not match a verbal offer. By providing something in writing you just might make it easier for the customer to get a better price somewhere else. But if you price is great and your overall value is superior, this should not become a major issue.

Communicate Clearly and Accurately

Regardless of where you might be in the sales process, clear and effective communication is of the utmost importance. This is because when communication is not clear and accurate and whenever interpretation or guesswork becomes involved, mistakes are bound to occur.

While most of us will agree on this, where some sales people might disagree is where I say that it is the sales person's responsibility to make sure that BOTH sides communicate clearly. That means that it is up to the sales person to make sure that the customer communicates clearly with them and that they communicate clearly with the customer.

But how do we make sure the customer communicate properly? Well, that is really easy. Whenever the customer says something that is not clear it is up to the salesperson to stop the conversation and ask questions designed to clarify what was said by the customer. If the customer is trying to be vague or evasive the sales person should ask questions to get specific answers to those questions.

While this will not stop the customer from lying outright or intentionally stop them from trying to deceive the salesperson, it will make the process much harder to do and also reveal a few warning signs along the way that may also help the salesperson.

When everyone is communicating clearly and accurately both parties can arrive at the same decisions by using the same information. There will be fewer mistakes, much less guesswork and an overall better chance of closing the deal in the best possible time frame.

Always keep in mind that the best results occur when accurate information is provided and understood by both parties not just one.

Make Eye Contact

When trying to close a sale, always make and keep eye contact with the customer. Not to the point where you are staring and making the customer feel uncomfortable but enough to establish a connection with that customer.

Making eye contact has the effect of establishing honesty and credibility in the eyes of the customer. People who refuse or avoid looking people in the eye when they talk appear to be "shifty" or dishonest. If a customer feels you are being less than honest you will lose any chance you might have had to close the sale at that time.

Creating eye contact also is a sign of confidence as well. When someone appears confident they are more readily believed by others. This helps you establish even more credibility in the eyes of the customer. Your self-confidence helps your customer feel more confident about you as well and they are more likely to believe in you and accept what you tell them.

Since confidence and integrity are important things that customers often look for, establishing that you possess those characteristics is important to the closing process.

Relate to the Customers Problems or Needs

People with problems or issues like it when they do not feel alone and often have the same issues in their lives. Or maybe the customer has a problem and they feel better when someone else they are talking to has already experienced that in their lives.

If you have experienced whatever problems or issues the customer currently has, use the personal experience to help close the sale. Tell them how you used the product to resolve the problem or what you did to make it better. Not only will this make the customer feel better but the personal information and advice you give them will be very much appreciated as well. Often this kind of information is not available anywhere else.

Understand, however, that you can show empathy without admitting guilt or taking responsibility. There is a distinct difference between empathy and sympathy. Telling someone you have been through a problem is much different than telling someone you are responsible for it!

Even if you are not selling something to the customer at this point but can help them in other ways, do it. People tend to remember who helped them in the past and will come back to purchase other products in the future. It is like building goodwill to pay you back on a future purchase.

A Personal Recommendation

Assuming the customer likes you and has faith in you, a personal recommendation can mean the difference between closing the sale and have the customer walk out without buying.

Customers know that you cannot always believe what is written on the package or stated in a commercial or other advertisement. They understand that claims are often exaggerated and that some of what they hear and read is almost total BS!

But if they have faith in your and you can deliver a personal recommendation based on your own use of the product that can carry a lot of weight.

Even if you share comments made by other customers as to how they felt about the product that could be information they might not be able to get anywhere else either.

Any recommendation you can provide just might be the final piece to the puzzle and could result in the closing of the sale. But even if it isn't the final piece it still helps build goodwill and confidence in the product in the eyes of the customer.

Testimonials

Much along the same lines as a personal recommendation, written or video testimonials can also have an impact on whether or not a customer is going to buy the product from you right now.

But beware that some customers do not believe the accuracy of a testimonial and for good reason. That is because some testimonials are just advertisements in disguise made by someone paid by the company to give a great review of the product. In this regard testimonials might work against you if they appear to over the top or too good to be true.

Be Personable

Though you would never know it from the way some salespeople act, customers like to purchase products from people that they like. Building a rapport with the customer is one of the most important parts of customer service and also sales techniques.

If you come off as personable and someone the customer can identify or relate to, you will have a much better chance of closing the sales than a stand-offish or obnoxious person does. After all, don't you like to deal with pleasant people more than obnoxious ones?

This generally becomes more important as the prices of the products goes higher. The personality of a car salesman or real estate agent becomes more of a factor than how the cashier treats you when you buy a loaf of bread. For minor purchases convenience is king. But then again, you don't have to close a sale for a loaf of bread. But for a car or a home, you most certainly do.

You do not have to be the customer's best friend or laugh at all their jokes or anything like that. But you need to be friendly and outgoing and appear to take a general interest in what the customer says and what their needs are. The customer doesn't have to feel the need to invite you home for dinner but they should like dealing with you throughout the sales process.

Interestingly enough this is where some sales teams fall short when it comes to the closer role. The salesman designated as the closer is often the person who comes in with the smile that's too big and the laugh that's too loud and the sales pitch that is just a bit too hard.

This is a turn-off for many customers. Fortunately, you are seeing less and less of this as these businesses appear to be finally getting the message.

Don't Be Afraid to Ask for the Sale

Many sales people are hesitant to ask for the sale thinking that this make them appear too high pressured in the eyes of the customer. But the reality is that the closer MUST ask for the sale at some point to nudge the customer into making a decision. Otherwise the closing process can go on and on without an end in sight.

You can make statements such as "Can I write you up for the blue model?" or "Would you like to pay cash or charge it?" or "We have two in stock right now. Would you like one?"

If you do that once or twice throughout the closing process that is not high pressure sales. That is just doing your job. But the reality is that if you don't go and ask for the sale many times you won't get it. So pick your spots, choose your approach carefully and ask for the sale. Any times you probably are going to get it.

Don't Be Scared to Ask Again

As they always say, if at first you don't succeed, try, try again. When trying to close a sale, you are often going to be rebuffed on your first attempt.

There might be objections to overcome, issues to discuss and several other obstacles to be removed before the customer will purchase from you. All of that is OK. You just have to be patient. Eliminate the obstacles and try again.

Easy ways to ask for the sale a second or third time might be: "All right, I was able to get you a 10% discount like you asked. How would you like to pay for this today?" or "OK, we seem to have addressed your concerns about buying today so Can I get the warehouse to bring the product out to your car?" or "I think we have addressed all your concerns. I hope I was able to put you at ease about purchasing today. Can I write you up and have your product brought out?"

The fact is, if you don't ask for the sale you are not as likely to get it. But ask nicely and do not ask again if nothing has changed. If the customer has concerns and objections and they are not addressed, do not ask them if they are ready to buy yet. That will just anger the customer. If conditions change, ask for the sale. If conditions do not change, don't ask again until they do change.

Stay with Your Customer

Many times salesmen will move from customer to customer so that they can close several sales and earn several commissions instead of just one.

While that certainly is understandable, when trying to close a sale you should stay with your customer until they make their decision.

When you leave a customer for whatever reason, you are making it easy for them to leave. While I do not mean we should hold anyone hostage or force them to stay, I am not saying you should make it easier for them to leave either.

Second, customers may develop questions and those questions can lead to not purchasing unless you are there to answer those questions and put the customer at ease. If a question or concern is not addressed promptly the customer will either leave or just decide not to buy at this time. Your presence helps avoid that from happening.

Stay with your customer, answer their questions, ask questions of your own designed to uncover any further problems, issues or concerns and then ask for the sale. Never leave your customer alone to make that decision without you. I guarantee you will lose sales if you do so.

Even a Prospect Can Be Turned into a Buyer

It is fairly common for sales people to label someone a "prospect" once they get the feeling that this customer is not going to be a buyer. But the fact is ANY customer that has a need or a desire CAN be converted into a buyer if the situation is handled correctly.

Prospects turn into buyers when the characteristics of the sale make it advantageous to purchase now. In other words, if someone is interested in buying something next month, a lower price right now can turn that customer into a buyer right now.

For example, Mr. and Mrs. Bernard are looking to go on a cruise next year. There is no urgency so they are just looking right now. But if you can show them that there is a sale going on right now where they can save 25% plus get free drinks and a free on-ship credit, you could convince them to commit right now instead of waiting!

Anyone with a need or desire is a possible customer and sale. Don't label people just because of what they say. Instead, concentrate on what you can do (in a nice way, of course) to turn that Prospect into a buying customer. It can be done if you do it right!

Be Confident

A good salesman will appear confident and secure at least on the outside. They will feel competent in their product knowledge as well as the procedures and processes of the business. They will feel confident answering questions and arriving at the right resolution or direction.

Customers can sense when someone is unsure of what they are saying or when they are not sure how to handle a certain situation. When customers do not feel confident about their sales person. They also feel even less confident that they are receiving accurate information or the best deal possible. In some cases they may ask for another sales person.

The sales closer MUST have all the answers and know the limitations of what they can and can't do when it comes to closing a sale. If the closer makes a commitment, they must be absolutely certain that commitment will be approved and honored. You cannot go back on a commitment once it is made to a customer and expect anything good to come from it.

A good closer also has to "think on their toes" and be able to come up with innovative ways to capture the sale. This can only be done when the sales person knows what to do and how to handle certain situations. Then they can take swift action, impress the customer and close the sale.

Be Positive

Remember when we discussed the importance of painting that perfect picture in the minds of our customers? Well, that picture has to be a positive picture. There is absolutely no room for any negatives. Everything must be positive so that it creates a very positive image. Anything less will not help in closing the sale.

Being positive means describing everything the product CAN do while staying away from any negative unless they are asked about by the customer. That means talking the product up and comparing it favorably to the customer.

It also means using the right words as well. Use positive sounding words such as "can" and "will" and staying away from negative words such as "can't" and "won't". This is important because our brains do not like negative words because negative words usually mean we are going to get less than we wanted or expected. In some cases, our brains shut down completely after hearing a negative word!

If you have to address a negative, try and place a positive "spin" on it whenever possible. Do not lie or deceive the customer but try to make the product look and sound the most positive you possibly can. Remember, positives increase a positive perception and increase the urge to buy. Negatives do the exact opposite!

Smile

This is another one of those body language things that can make a big difference when it comes to dealing with customers. Approaching the customer with a smile on your face and a pleasant disposition can help reduce negative feelings or emotions and place the customer more at ease.

A smile is reassuring and disarming when it comes to how a person feels about you. After all it is much harder to yell or be angry at someone who is smiling at you! Smiles also convey warmth and caring as well. A smile is well known to draw people together while a frown is known to drive people further apart.

A smile is also viewed as a positive response while a frown has a whole lot of negative connotations. Since we want the entire sales process, including the closing, to be as positive as possible we want our facial expressions to add to the positive feelings not take away from them.

Take Your Time & don't Rush!

The sales process, when done correctly, cannot be rushed. Good closing takes time and patience. When a sale has to be closed that means there are remaining issues that must be dealt with and sometimes uncovered first. That means spending the time to ask the right questions and then evaluating the answers to determine the best next steps. You should not rush through this part of the process.

Whenever you try to rush through something and the customer realizes this, they do not feel as important to the salesman and the business as they should. Since one of the most important aspects of the sales process involves feeling important and appreciated, rushing through things sends the wrong message to the customer.

Rushing through also increases the potential of missing important information because you didn't take the time to ask the right questions or to listen to whatever the customer is telling you. Whenever either of these things occur the potential for confusion and wrong decisions goes up dramatically.

Don't worry about other customers when you are dealing with someone already. Hopefully there are other salespeople around to help them while you continue to help your customer. This sends the right message to the customer and helps reaffirm their importance to the company.

It is also a sign of respect when you give people the time they deserve. It shows them that you value their time and their business. It also shows them that you are willing to listen to what they have to say and that you are also willing to spend the time to make sure they get what they need when they need it.

With so little attention being spent on customers these days sometimes spending just a little more time with a customer can result in significant sales to those who do!

Sell Value not Price

Here is one area where so many sales people totally and completely miss the boat.

They try to close a sale concentrating on just the sales price and not on the total value of the purchase to the customer.

While price is important, many people do not consider prices to be at the top of their list of priorities. They value the suitability of the product for their application to be important as well as convenience and overall customer experience higher than the selling price in many situations.

Besides price there are other items that factor into the total value as well. Convenience, peace of mind, free delivery, in home service and other extras sometimes have a greater impact than price for some customers. You need to "sell" those extras as well.

Just something as simple as a Saturday or Sunday delivery might mean that a customer doesn't have to take time off from work and this could mean far more than anything else. But unless you make them aware of the weekend deliveries, it might also mean totally nothing.

When trying to close a deal and make a sale, including EVERYTHING that might have a value to that customer. ANYTHING that you or your business offers that your competition doesn't should be made clear to your customer. Whether it has value or not can be left up to the customer. But often times the total package can have a LOT more value than just the selling price.

That is also why it makes sense to offer more value added services than your competition does. If they offer one thing and you can offer better, make that known to your customer. If you offer less, than you competition, consider improving your offering so it compares more favorably.

The value of your overall package is something that has a direct impact on how many sales you close and how many people walk out. But if you close on total value instead of just price, you will find it easier to close more sales than just talking up price and nothing else.

Follow-Up with Customers after the Meeting

Many sales people subscribe to the thought "Out of sight out of mind" and that is a shame because many a sale has been closed or won back by keeping in contact with the customer. That is because sometimes people become so busy they do not have the time to come back in or other things take over and they totally forget about other things.

But sometimes just making a follow-up phone call to see if the customer has any other questions or to make them aware that the product they were looking at is going to be on sale next week can really recapture some sales. It is just a way of bringing the issue back up front and seeing if the customer is still interested.

Or, you can call your customers with an upgraded offer or some kind of incentive to get them to come back in and purchase. Many times this is all that is needed to get things back on track and restart the process. The incentive doesn't have to be much. Just enough to rekindle interest in the product. It might also help sway them back to you if they were considering buying from someone else.

Provide Incentives

One particularly effective closing technique is to offer additional incentives to close the deal right then and there. Those incentives can range from a limited time price reduction to free accessories or free value added services. We talked about selling value instead of just price and this is one way to add significant value to the offer and close the sale right now.

But when you do this you have to make sure you do it in such a way that you don't appear sleazy or dishonest. Do not overinflate the value of your bonuses or incentive easier. Believe me when I tell you that most customers do not believe that the free power supply you are offering really costs $99.95! Be open and honest.

For example, you might say something like:

"Mrs. Owens, I know you like the product but are still unsure about whether or not you can afford it. If it will help you make a decision, I can offer you a 10% discount if you buy it now.

Maybe that will make it easier for you to afford. But I cannot extend that offer after you leave the store. I apologize for that."

Or:

"Mrs. Owens, this products is going on sale next week so I don't want you to be upset that you paid more for it now than it will cost you next week. If you want to purchase it now I can give you the sale price right now instead of waiting a week. Would that work for you?"

Or:

"Mrs. Owens, I am sure this is the perfect product for what you need and I really want to see you walk out with it today. I'm sure you will be thrilled with it. Because of that, I would like to give you a free accessory of your choice as a way of saying thank you for purchasing today. But please understand that I can only do that today not tomorrow or at any time in the future."

Closing Techniques Summary

How to best close a sales is going to depend upon the particular product, your customer and the reasons why they are considering purchasing that product at this time. Naturally the more urgent the need the more likely your customer is to buy. But if the need is not really there you might have to convince them to buy and buy now.

That is where all of the previously mentioned techniques will come into play. You will probably wind up using more than one of these techniques though sometimes you might only need one. But the key is not just in the technique you will use, it is deciding which technique is the best in that situation.

Put yourself in the customers shoes and ask yourself how you would feel in the same situation and what you would like to see happen or done at this point in time. Think about your needs and how you would like them addressed. Since our customers are people too, chances are you will want pretty much what your customer wants. At least it will give you a pretty good starting point.

So start off doing a quick evaluation then choose the best approach or approaches. Then use those techniques and approaches and go from there. Do not think that one approach will work for everyone because everyone is different. Just make a choice, evaluate the results and then either keep going or change your approach.

On-Line Closing Strategies

With so much business being done on-line these days any book on how to close a sales call would be remiss if it didn't touch on how to close internet based sales. This is also important because internet sales is a very different process when it comes to closing sales.

When you make a sale over the internet, unless you use a live chat, the sales process largely exists on the webpage itself in the form or sales copy, videos and pictures. There is no direct human interaction or the ability to ask questions or opinions.

Because of this careful attention has to be paid to how sales copy is written to that all common questions and concerns are addressed in that sales copy. This is crucial because lingering doubts that still exist after everything is seen and listened to can stop the sales process immediately.

Depending on where you are purchasing your products and the type of products you are purchasing, closing the sale can be attempted in several different ways. Unfortunately, most of these way often include false claims of scarcity or over inflated bonuses and other similar practices. Since people expect these and are wise to the techniques will probably have to be better and a lot more discreet to be effective.

In this chapter we are going to go over a few of the most common internet closing methods just to give you an idea of what they are and why they are supposed to work. This is done mostly so that you understand the psychology behind them so that you can craft or create your own closing techniques on your web site.

Keep in mind that these are just the most common closing techniques and that new ones are added all the time as new ideas come about and new technology permits certain actions off of our web sites. But regardless of the changes that may or may not come, the prevailing reason behind then has not changed.

Websites look and read the way they do because that is the way they have to be to create sales. In other words, those sites work and they convert. So lets' take a look at some of the most common internet closing techniques and why they work.

Scarcity

This is one of the most common sales closing techniques found online when it comes to certain products. The "scarcity model" tells the reader that there are limited number of these products available and once they are gone that's it. They will never be available again.

This preys on the fear within the customer's mind that they had better act now or they risk never being able to get the product again in the future. If it is something they really want, they will buy it now to avoid missing out. This can be a powerful incentive in the mind of the customer.

The reality is that usually there are no limited quantities or if they are limited the limit is so high that it will never be reached. So that limited edition flying pig mug you fell in love with might be available in limited quantities but that limit might be 15 million!

People are used to this and it can be difficult to get some of your customers to believe this is really limited in availability. Which is sad because some products really are limited and customer might really miss out if they do not act right them while they are available!

Limited Time Offer

This is something that is kind of a new twist on an old but effective idea.

With technology now making it easy to include a "count-down" clock on your web pages, people who want a certain product now see time clicking down in front of their eyes.

This is effective because not only is the customer made aware that this is a limited time offer but that clock actually shows the minutes and second ticking away. Depending on the time left the urge to buy can be small or create a full blown panic as the time clicks down to zero!

This is another form of the scarcity or limited availability closing technique that is designed to create a high level of urgency. As we said, it is effective even though sometimes the urgency is manufactured and not real at all.

Escalating Prices

This is one of those closing techniques that is used almost exclusively on the internet. In this technique, prices go up either as time goes by or as a certain number has been sold. Regardless of how they go up it also creates a sense of urgency with the customer.

For example, a website might tell the customer that a certain product is currently selling for $10 but every time 5 units are sold the price will increase by a dollar. Or, the starting price will be $10 but the price will go up $1 every hour until the full price of $29. 00 is reached.

This creates a powerful incentive to buy because no one wants to pay more for something than they have to. But this really only works well when you give people advanced notice such as when releasing a new product. You put a message on your website stating the product will start selling on such a date and time and that it will rise in price according to time or sales.

This is more effective when the prices are at their lowest because that is when the potential savings are at their highest. As the price increases, the savings are less but there still will be a certain amount of incentive.

This also works very well when you want to get a lot of sales very soon after release. This can help establish a product and get reviews or testimonials to help further promote and establish the product in the marketplace.

Pre-Launch Discounting

This is where you cut the price of a new product before it is formally introduced or placed on sale. This saves the customers money which is an incentive to purchase now rather than later. You can either send them the product right away or take pre-orders to be filled when the product is actually placed on sale.

But keep in mind that people like to get the materials as quickly as possible so making them wait might reduce the number of orders you receive. People are funny that way. They want to save money but they still do not like to wait.

Another variation of this is to include a bonus or other incentive to pre-order the product before it is launched. Again, this creates an illusion of getting more value for their money even though the actual bonus might be worth little or nothing.

Incentive & Bonuses

Speaking of bonuses, the offering of a bonus has become some prominent when selling certain types of product it is more or less expected. This even though the supposed value of these bonuses is often so inflated that it is laughable.

This past week I saw someone offer a bonus supposedly worth $6,000 if you bought a $27 product from their affiliate link. Now why on earth would someone give you stuff legitimately worth $6,000 in exchange for a $10 affiliate commission????

The thing with internet bonuses, or any other bonus for that matter is that the value is subjective. I can write a report and place a $495 price tag on it but that doesn't mean it is worth that much or that anyone would be stupid enough to pay me that much for it. But yet there you see that figure listed as the value for this "bonus".

Look, most people are not that stupid and will see through inflated prices and overstated values and this might harm your sales. But at the same time you have to compete with these guys and their $6,000 bonus package so you have to weigh your options. While I said that most people will spot over valued items, some will not and really believe they are getting $6,000 worth of stuff for their $27.

Fear

Whether or not you are selling on-line or through your retail business fear is a very strong motivator when it comes to deciding what to purchase. If you have a product that will provide safety or peace of mind then it might not be hard to get people to buy it from you.

When it comes to closing the sale personal and family safety are powerful reasons to buy as well. Most people would do or buy anything if it would help safeguard themselves or their families.

But be careful when using fear as a motivator because it if appears that you are preying on people's fear to make a sale they will resent you for it. There is a difference between a real threat and a manufactured one. You should realize this because your customers surely will.

Testimonials

Here is something that sometimes works very well while other times it doesn't help a bit. Testimonials on websites are widely suspicious as far as how real and truthful they are. Wild claims and phony names often accompany these testimonials which are actually sales pitches in disguise. Sometimes the pictures do not even match the names used. They are just pictures taken off the web from somewhere and pasted into the web page!

If you have real and honest testimonials and they accurately represent what the product can do and how the products actually work, then feel free to use them. If they look and sound real people might believe them. But do not create your own testimonials and post them somewhere and claim they are unsolicited. There are laws against doing that sort of thing.

Sales Copy

Sales copy is important regardless of what kind of business you are in but on a website, it is downright critical. As we said before, selling on line is done almost totally by the words that are written on the webpage. There are no salesman to talk to the customers and no way for questions to be answered.

So the sales copy must be compelling and give plenty of reasons for the customer to buy.

It must be descriptive and it must create that vivid and lifelike picture in the mind of the customer. And it must do that while the customer is still interested.

Written sales copy has to capture the attention and interest of the reader within a few seconds or the customer will leave and go to another site. For this reason internet sales copy usually contains a bit of hype and over stated claims just to capture the interest of the customer and to keep them engaged. As we said, there is no salesperson to step in and re-engage the customer when they get bored and ready to leave.

So the sales copy must introduce the product, detail its features and benefits, let the customer know what problems or needs that it solves and then attempt to close the sale by driving that message home with added benefits and a few bonuses thrown in besides.

This is not an easy process and skilled copywriters earn high salaries just for writing sales copy that leads to sales. So as long as you can do so honestly and ethically, write compelling sales copy that will produce the same desired effect as you get when you are talking to someone face to face.

But as I just said, do it honestly and ethically. There are rules for this as well. And you should follow them.

Money Back Guarantees

Perhaps the most important thing when you are selling anything on-line is to offer a no questions asked, money back guarantee. This is because whenever people buy something online, unless it is a well- known product that they can see, feel and touch locally, they have no idea what the product is really like. So there is always a degree of uncertainty whenever a customer is thinking about purchasing something online.

Another factor is that when you purchase something locally, you can go back to the store when something goes wrong or whenever you need to return or exchange the product. Not so easy when you purchase something online.

Because of these two things offering a no questions asked guarantee is not only recommended, it is downright a necessity. People are always going to buy from places where they feel safe and secure and this warranty accomplishes most of that. While there still might be some hesitancy, it will be reduced by the guarantee.

Contact Information

If you want to have people purchase from your online business you are going to have to reassure them that this is a legitimate business. You can partially accomplish this by placing contact information on your website so people will have a way of communicating with you.

This contact information can be in the form of an e-mail address or an actual phone number. Whatever method you choose you really need to have some way of getting in touch with you. This would be for returns, defective products or just when a customer has questions.

If people search your site and find nothing in the form of how to contact someone they are really going to be discouraged from purchasing from your site. At least have an e-mail address for people to contact you. Then, of course, monitor that e-mail inbox and answer every e-mail.

Payment Options

Closing sales also becomes easier when people can pay for products with well-known and trusted payment options. Credit cards are a necessity and for certain products and services an online payment option such as PayPal will come in handy as well.

It is much easier to close a sale when the payment method is respected and when it offers additional protection against the product and the business selling it. Offering multiple respected payment services also helps create the impression that yours is a well-established and trusted business.

Mailing Lists & Follow-Up

If you can, try and capture the names and e-mail addresses of those people contacting you with questions and other matters. Then you can use this list to follow-up with these customers and try and close a few sales. You can also use your mailing list to make people aware of new products, specials and other sales that you are running.

When it comes to using your list as follow-ups to inquires make sure not to over burden or abuse your subscribers. I always recommend no more than one e-mail a week unless you are running a sale or special event which can justify an extra e-mail or two.

If you really want to close more sales and use e-mail to help accomplish that, you want to make sure your e-mails are actually read. The best way to do that is to include some valuable or worthwhile information inside every e-mail so your subscribers will eagerly open them to see what is in each new e-mail.

Offer product information, reviews or some information you know will be of interest to your subscribers. That way these e-mails will not be seen as sales pitches but instead worthwhile information sources that are deserved to be read. Another benefit of these types of e-mails is that they might actually be saved or forwarded and might generate sales for you months, even a year or more later!

Always remember that e-mail is a fast and very economical way to keep in touch with customers.

But because of those same reasons, it is also among the most abused forms of communication as well. Therefore many customers simply delete e-mails without even reading them. But they will usually read the first one or two out of curiosity. If they see content that they feel has value or merit, they will keep reading. But if the e-mails you send are just selling item after item they will not continue to read your e-mails moving forward. Even if you change the content and start offering valuable information and content to your e-mails later on, people might never know that because they simply delete them without reading them.

Autoresponder Follow-Up

It is interesting to know that most people will not buy from a company on their first visit to their website. This is because the business is considered new to them and they have a lack of confidence in the website and business that needs to be overcome.

They might search under the business name to see what information comes up and if there are any complaints or any other information that can give them an idea of whether or not this is a reputable business or not. They might search around to see if other, more well-known businesses have the same products at the same prices and buy them there where they feel more comfortable.

Because of this we need to get the customer to come back to our site in the future, perhaps several times. We need to inspire confidence in the mind of the customer so that their lack of confidence is no longer the determining factor for their refusal to purchase. We do this by being pro-active and initiating contact ourselves.

An autoresponder is something we use in conjunction with our e-mail to automatically contact customers at regular intervals with information and other content designed to impress them and make them want to re-visit our website. The more they come back the more confidence they will develop in our business.

Sending a customer an e-mail a month or a week giving them information that they view as being positive about your business and the products you sell can be a powerful inducement to get them to close a sale and purchase a product from you.

The e-mails should be short, concise and provide content that is valuable and not related to selling anything to anyone. In fact, if you send out information based e-mails that people find helpful, they will be more responsive when you add a short sales pitch or two in up-coming e-mails.

Autoresponders can be programmed to send out these e-mails automatically at pre-determined intervals so that every time a name is added to your e-mail list they will start receiving these follow-up e-mails. This can be an easy way to keep in contact with the customer and keep your business in their mind when it comes to when they need to complete their purchase.

Improving Customer Engagement

Just like getting customers involved in face to face situations, customers are more likely to stay on your webpages and complete their purchases if you can find some way of engaging them in the process.

There are several ways that you can accomplish this. You can utilize surveys, contest, forms and other web elements designed to get the customers involved with your business. But keep in mind that the customer must see a value in doing so. Their time is valuable and you want to make sure they feel it is worth their while to get involved with your business website.

Customer engagement is important because it increases the time they remain on your site instead of getting bored and clicking off to the next website. Remember that it is much easier to go from site to site than it is to go from store to store so people leave websites much faster than they leave retail stores.

Closing Phrases

When it comes to closing a sale, some kind of verbal interaction is almost always part of the process. What we mean by that is that at some point in the process you are going to have to ask for the sale. Most customers will need that kind of push in order to buy.

But we usually just do not blurt out "Can I have this sale, please?" to the customer. Most of the time the question is a lot less direct and something that is contained within another question. Below are a few phrases you might use and how they accomplish asking for the sale without actually doing so.

You should also note that with the exception of the first question these are all positive questions indicating a benefit to the customer for taking action now. The first one, while dealing with a negative is designed to uncover any remaining concerns or issues so that they can be addressed and lead to the completion of the sale.

Here are some common closing phrases:

Is there anything about (the product or service) that you don't like?

This is designed to get the customer to give you any remaining concerns or issues that are preventing them from closing the sale. This is useful because you now have one last chance to remove these roadblocks from the process. When every issue or concern has been addressed, the customer will have no reason not to purchase. At this point your job is much easier and you can turn to another closing phrase to seal the deal.

What can I do to get you to purchase this today?

This is a somewhat blunt questions designed to get the customer to tell you what it will take to get them to buy today. Very often you can judge by their answers whether or not they are really interested in purchasing your product. If they give you a legitimate answer, you can proceed. If they give you some off the wall and exorbitant demand, they are not truly engaged.

What price would convince you to purchase today?

If much of your discussion up to this point have revolved around pricing, this question just puts it right out there when you ask what price will seal the deal for them today.

Keep in mind that some customers will throw a ridiculous number out there just to see your reaction. But at least that number can open the dialogue and hopefully result in a number that will help close the sale while making everyone happy.

So, would you like this delivered or would you prefer to take it with you?

Here you are not asking for the order specifically but instead asking whether or not they want to take it with them or have it delivered. Often times this kind of shrouded request is all that it will take to get the customer to make the commitment.

When should we get started?

Another phrase that kind of assumes the sale is closed and moves on to talking about when to get started. This asks for the sale in a roundabout way that can be very effective when the customer is close to making their decision.

I think of the two products, this one is the best. Which one would you prefer?

Sometimes when you cannot choose between two products and the customer continues to "waffle" back and forth, asking them to let you know which product is better will help you understand which product you should concentrate on.

This can be very helpful when dealing with people who have a hard time making any kind of decision. This phrase also leads to more customer engagement as well because you are asking them for their opinion.

I would hate to see you miss out on this product at this price.

If there really is a great price on what they are looking to purchase there is no reason why this should not become part of the closing. You can add "You do realize that you can save a lot of money by buying this today." If you wait it is going to cost you at least $100 more if you wait.

If you sign today, I can give you XXX at no additional cost.

When a customer is sitting on the fence and just not sure if they want to buy or not, offering an additional incentive can sometimes push the customer over to the "buy side". You might offer them free delivery, a free accessory or some kind of store credit or gift card to get them to commit. The gift card is a great idea because it forces them to come back and buy something else which usually will be more expensive than the gift card anyway.

Will that be cash or charge?

Here is a way to ask for the sale without actually asking for the sale! Asking whether it will be cash or charge assumes the sale is closed and it will be up to the customer to stop the process. Very often the customer who was very close to buying will just allow the process to continue. It is also a very effective way of trying to put an end to the process rather than allowing it to drag on and on due to indecision.

Are you interested in a few accessories as well?

Nothing is better than closing a sale unless it can be closing a larger sale! Never let a sale go through without offering or asking if there are any other accessories or items that the customer might want. If something requires batteries and they are not included, ask if they want to buy them.

If there are accessories that most people buy, of if any of those accessories are required for the product to do what the customer wants it to do then it would be inexcusable not to offer or recommend those accessories. Imagine how the customer might feel if they get their purchase home and find out they need something else in order to make it work!

Most customers will appreciate being informed of other items that might be needed as long as you are not badgering them with item after item after item.

Building Relationships

Now that we have gone through a few sales basics and some effective sales techniques, let's briefly touch on something not directly related to closing sales but still will have a significant impact on that process. We are going to discuss the importance and benefits of establishing relationships with your customers. Because those salesman who take the time and make the effort to establish these relationships are much more productive and much more successful.

Establishing relationships with your customers accomplishes several things. Here are just a few advantages to having positive relationships with all your customers:

Increased Confidence

When you develop a relationship with a customer that is based on trust and you helping them effectively and properly in the past, that customer develops more confidence with you over that time.

The more you help them and the more they value your input, the more confident they become that you are someone they have confidence in. This is important because there are so many sales people and businesses out there who are interest in their customers only for the money.

Increased Trust

The more confident you are with someone the more likely you are going to be to trust and believe in what they are telling you. This can become hugely important as time goes by when you want to close a sale. If the customer knows you and trusts you, they will listen to you more and take your suggestions to heart. This almost always has a positive impact on your ability to close more and larger sales.

This also helps when you are in the product selection stage and you are trying to convince the customer to purchase another product instead of the one they came if for. Maybe the product is a better fit or a better all-around product but your customer might not believe you if they do not know you.

Improved Communication

Everyone communicates better with people they know and trust. Suspicion is less, barriers come down and meaningful communication starts almost from the very beginning.

You also have much less of a chance that the customer is going to come in angry with you so you will not have to spend a lot of time calming the customer back down. In some cases, you might even be given the benefit of the doubt and be able to use that to your advantage.

Since communication is always better, more accurate and most efficient when everyone is calm and happy, having a relationship with the person you are talking with usually helps a great deal.

Fewer Roadblocks during the Sales Process

Customers that have relationships with salespeople do not have to take the time to feel comfortable with each other or to determine whether or not the salesman is honestly looking out for the customer or not. Since much of the initial sales process involves eliminating suspicion and feeling comfortable with each other, you will find that you will close more sales in less time with customers who already know and trust you.

More Sales

Customers that have a relationship with a sales person are far more likely to come back again in the future to buy more products and services from that same salesperson.

Not only will they feel more comfortable with someone they are familiar with, their confidence that they are going to be treated well brings them back for more most of the time.

People are creatures of habit and once they feel comfortable with someone or a business they tend to keep coming back until there is a reason not to. So if you develop a relationship and keep adding positive experiences to it you should have a customer for many years to come. Of course, if you stop treating the customer right those same customers can leave at any time.

More Positive Word of Mouth Advertising

One of the most frustrating things for sales people is to have a customer walk through the door and ask to speak to a specific salesperson. Often that means a potential loss of commission and sales. But people don't ask for someone specifically without a reason. They do it because that salesman has a relationship with someone who recommended them.

I worked in a business where other salesmen were very angry with another salesman. They all claims that he was stealing their commissions. But the fact really was that those customer who asked for him specifically never met him before.

They were recommended by someone who did have a relationship with him over the years. This didn't happen with the other salesmen because they were not interested in developing relationships at all. They just wanted to run from one customer to another so they could earn more commissions.

But when customers already know you and feel comfortable with you and when you treat them right, they become your sales ambassadors. They tell family and friends about you and the service you gave them. They tell you how pleased they were and how you stepped up to make sure their best interests were protected. By doing this they have opened the doors to even more sales by handing you new customers on a silver platter.

How do you Build Relationships with your Customers?

Building relationships takes time and it take effort and commitment. Any salesman can write up a sale and collect the money. But the salesman who is also willing to create a relationship at the same time will create customers for life. In other words, you invest time and effort now in return for additional sales tomorrow.

Here are a few easy things you can do to develop relationships with your customers:

Treat them Well

First and foremost, you must treat your customers well and give them a high quality customer experience. You must be pleasant and helpful and not rush the customers or make them feel like they are an imposition. If you can help them with something, then help them. If they need something, get it for them. If they have questions, then answer them or get them the answers.

In other words, just do the things you would appreciate being done for you.

Watch out for their Interests

We all know what our customers want and if we don't hopefully we will take the time to ask them. But once we know what is important, great salesmen look for ways to give them as much of what they want as possible. They understand the long term relationship is far more important than wringing out one extra dollar from the current sale.

This is something so simple and so easy to understand it is absolutely amazing that everyone doesn't follow this simple premise. But they don't so that leaves the door wide open for you to step in and steal that customer away.

Communicate with Them

Stay in touch with your customers. Make them aware of upcoming sales or when there is a price cut on something you think they might be interested in. Send them an e-mail announcing a sale or better yet, send them an e-mail on their birthday just wishing them a Happy Birthday! No sales pitch, no hype, just a birthday wish. If you want to go the extra mile, throw in a discount coupon or some other birthday "gift" for them in the e-mail.

Not only will this make them happy and pleased that you remembered them but the gift will also bring them back into the store where you will be able to help them again and further develop that relationship.

Fight for Them

If a customer has a problem, help them even though there is no commission or sale involved. If they are having trouble, fight for them. If they are in a dispute that you feel is a legitimate one, be an advocate.

Don't be one of those salesmen who won't do a damned thing if there is no commission involved. Cultivate the relationship whenever the opportunity presents itself. You might not see a commission today but you are going to see many more in the future if you do the right thing now.

Appreciate Them

One of the things customer appreciate most is feeling appreciated. So take a moment to thank them for their business. Tell them you appreciate their business and for them coming back to you. Make them feel wanted as well. Remember that your business would not be in business if it were not for your customers. Make sure they know that and that you appreciate them coming back to you instead of someone else.

Conclusion

Closing sales is something that is not difficult to do but it does take a bit of practice. Not only do you have to know the correct words to say and when to say them, you have to know what the customer is really looking for and what objections might still exist.

So you have to be part salesman, part detective and part psychologist in order to be a good closer. But please don't be intimidated by this because we all have the ability to become good closers as long as we don't mind talking to people and asking a few questions.

The most successful closers, and regular sales people, are the ones who are personable and who really have the customer's best interests at heart.

These are the salesmen who might not appear to close every sale but at the end of the month they are always among the sales leaders.

Whenever you are with a customer, whether you feel that they are in buying mode or not, remember that every sale has the potential to be closed right then and there. It might be more difficult, sometimes almost impossible in some cases, but there is always a chance if the situation is handled properly and effectively.

This book has attempted to give you the knowledge and background to enable you to hit the ground running when it comes to closing sales. You might make a mistake or two in the beginning but over time you will develop the skills and instincts all good closers have. When that happen you will see your success rate sky rocket and you will become much more productive in everything you do.

It is not hard and it does not take a lot of time to learn and use what is contained in this book. But take your time and really understand what you are reading. You don't get points for reading the fastest. You get your points in your results and those come when you really do understand the content and techniques in the book.

Good luck and happy closing!

For more information on
entrepreneur Skills,
please go to our website at:

http://www.entrepreneurinstitute.
com

For more information on Customer
Service and The Customer Service
Training Institute,

please go to our website at:

http://www.infowhse.com